CIVIL TWILIGHT

CIVIL
TWILIGHT

POEMS

JEFFREY SCHULTZ

An Imprint of HarperCollins*Publishers*

HarperCollins books may be purchased for educational, business, or sales promotional use. For information please e-mail the Special Markets Department at SPsales@harpercollins.com.

FIRST EDITION

Designed by Suet Yee Chong

Library of Congress Cataloging-in-Publication Data has been applied for.

ISBN 978-0-06-267898-0

17 18 19 20 21   LSC   10 9 8 7 6 5 4 3 2 1

CONTENTS

ACKNOWLEDGMENTS

Thanks to the editors and staffs of the following publications, in which some of the poems from this collection originally appeared, sometimes in slightly different form:

Academy of American Poets' Poem-a-Day: "Habeas Corpus"
TriQuarterly: "Civil Twilight"
Southern Indiana Review: "Offering of Two Burning Calves"

Selections from "Resolution in Loving Memory of Sky & Gooseflesh" appeared in *Fogged Clarity,* and "Habeas Corpus" was anthologized in *The Manifesto Project*.

Thanks to David St. John, Beth Dial, Daniel Halpern, and the National Poetry Series, and to Bridget Read and everyone at Ecco and HarperCollins.

For their support, guidance, and friendship, thanks to my family, to Chuck and Dianne Hanzlicek, Peter Everwine, Connie and John Hales, Dixie Salazar and Jon Veinberg, Franny Levine, Pimone Triplett, James Leveque, Allison Perkins, Cyndy Holder, Adam Van Arsdale and Hélène Bilis, Giri Iyengar,

Lorie Goodman and Bob Cook, Jonas Lerman and Kristin Mjolsnes, Jane Rodeheffer, Maire Mullins, Michael Ditmore, F. Douglas Brown, Marty Williams, Carlos Ramírez, and Genny Moore.

Thanks to all my wonderful students, most especially Matthew Jones, Rachal Marquez, Levi Osburn, Alex Free, Ben Keoseyan, and Kami Bates, for humoring and enabling me.

For reading versions of these poems in progress and for their tremendous encouragement, solidarity, and comradeship, thanks to Anna Tullis, Ben Evans, Jordan Straubel, Aaron Schott, Joel Wood, Brian Simoneau, and Isaac Randel. Special thanks in this regard to Joshua Robbins, Megan Levad, Alana Grambush, Hillary Eaton, Garrett Hongo, Haley Laningham, and George Kovalenko.

For her absolutely unwavering support and for her unerring eye and ear and heart and mind, as well as for putting up with me from day to day, thanks most of all to Leah Hanzlicek, to whom this book would be dedicated, would such a dedication not seem so deliriously awful.

In memoriam: Ruth and Vernon Schultz, always radically themselves.

CIVIL

TWILIGHT

STARE DECISIS
ET NON QUIETA MOVERE

History? We don't know. We'll all be dead.

—George W. Bush

If, our irises unflexing, their novae's bursts succumbing to apertures'

Black, our pupils becoming willing to admit what they might admit,

However insufficient, however insignificant in that scheme of things

We imagine must even now unfold somehow beyond our understanding,

Beyond us, if to look up widening into the night sky and stare at the stars,

Those grains of salt scattered across obsidian, those pale fires,

Those distant repositories of whatever we put there, those whatever,

Is in fact to stare into the past, then to live in the city is to live without

History. Or is at least to live blind to it, mistake it for something else,

Some cobble exposed as the asphalt chips, little by little, away,

Some incompleteness that yet offers us a sense of completion, a sense

Some something must have led to all this, some strategic planning

Commission's guiding hand, some intelligent designer's intelligent design.

Best to worry over it no further, best to not ask *why* regarding the *this*ness

Of this, the *that*ness of that, best face facts: go down that wrong road

And your FOIA requests' denials will drag on for years, and you've only
So many left, you know, so many years before the Municipality of Matter
Not Tied Up for the Moment in the Operation of Any Consciousness
Comes to file its own claim—its eminent domain, your body—; besides,
The legal fees will ruin you and, well, don't you want to enjoy life? *Let it,*
As they say, *lie.* Which it does, as per precedent, as we would expect.
And you try, Lord knows you try to act right, keep things simple,
Show up to meetings mostly on time and looking like you might belong,
Like you're committed to the institution and to its mission, though not,
You know, too committed, nothing that would arouse suspicion you're
Anything but perfectly professional, perfectly detached, the causes you call
Your own really only things to pass time that might pass otherwise unfilled.
But the idea was that we would not be contained by what contains us,
That we could walk outside and gaze upward and open ourselves not
To some speckled nothing, not to the city's orangey haze reflected back
But, because the biconvex curvature of our eyes' lenses is, finally,
Our curvature, open ourselves instead out to our own likeness, widened
And clarified by time and distance, that against that endless unpatterning
A field of meaningful points might be plotted. And though, sure,
We can check the *Weekly*'s horoscope, read that the Great Dog has ransacked
The House of Gemini, read in the police blotter that it's on a spree, tearing
Through each house in turn, shredding the archives—which anyway
Were only ever accessible to initiates, so investigators shrug—and soiling
The rugs, read in the features that its now-missing owners beat it as a pup
And that its story has been optioned for a film, it's far from what you feel
Was promised, far from your good behavior's just reward. So you try again
To think things through, try to remember at each moment that everyone
Else exists and is not trying to think of you thinking of them, and that that
Has always been the case, even and especially before you were there to try

And to fail at it, a failure which has now left you stunned aware

Of the little space that makes up your own consciousness, which gazes

Up at a nothing that reflects only its own blank vastness back to you,

And then even those things that catch at the corners of your eyes

Seem suddenly very genuinely perched at perception's precipitous edge,

And it's that—the violent wonder of being—that you would want

To come to understand and press outward until it could be called a history

Of something, a history that, if you could imagine it fully and know it—you

Along with simultaneously everyone—would be what we could call hope.

And it's this last part, which amounts to despair's almost measurable presence,

That leaves you bed-bound and despairing. Your doctor, making note

Of your case history, making note of the insurance company's reluctance—

And this has little to do with you, but ever since the courts upheld

Corporations' right to marry they seem hardly interested in us,

Seem consumed by their family lives, by raising their young dividends

Up right, our future upright corporate citizens—to prescribe for you

The different world in which you could actually live, making note that,

Of this summer's dog days you've now spent three massacres or two weeks—

Depending, of course, on whether you've converted to the newly instituted

Second Amendmentarian calendar or are still among the Gregorians,

With their quaint memories of feast days and cool weather seasons,

With their old idea of existence as unending cycle, a natural enough thing

To believe in before existence revealed its spiral down toward catastrophe—,

But anyway however you want to measure it, you've been essentially

Immobilized for a good while now and what your doctor suggests

In lieu of fulfillment is at least making sure to get out a little bit,

Certain of course you've first massaged a sufficient quantity of sunscreen,

The oxybenzone in which causes coral reefs and by extension, eventually,

Everything to wither and disappear, into your skin, because you want to be

Safe as you can be, your doctor says, don't want to take unnecessary risks,

Want to be able to pass through the world without falling in love with it:

To move without being moved. To admit nothing, least of all delusion,

The admission of which triggers a series of red flags and automated alarms

That will, finally, result in the Corporation's notification: supper interrupted,

He dabs his lips with his napkin and excuses himself, apologizes to the wife,

Smiles quickly at the children before heading back to his study to dial up

His old school friend the State, who mobilizes the necessary resources,

Which are not inconsiderable. Best to listen to good sense; best rest easy.

But thing is it told us the dogs would be sleeping and that we need only

Tread lightly, keep quiet, not make too much a fuss over anything.

There's a point at which, however against its will, however involuntary,

Even a lie will widen suddenly to admit those things it might admit,

Widen and reflect back those images of us it has so long concealed:

That, for one, we can't even walk anywhere anymore without worrying over

What bears down on us. Breeding has seen to it that the muzzle can press

So hard up against chain-link it bleeds; the will to survive has been distilled

Down to a form of self-sacrifice; it's become another form entirely:

All violence and no wonder. Wonder, a valuable waste product, is sold

For use in the production of films and integrated weapons systems.

When history extracted the teeth from the gums and lashed them to sticks

So that the mouth could be thrown at our enemies, so that the mouth,

So that what of it pierces and tears, could be abstracted from itself,

Lessening thereby the risk of blood-borne illness, yes, it allowed us,

More importantly, to feel and consider the calm refinement of civility,

A feeling that the worst of things happen beyond the bounds of us,

Happen, somehow, beyond us, without us, out in a world as wide

As it is unimaginable. Which is why the Demiurge is busy upgrading

Broadband access. The Demiurge desires that all our images be crisp

And archivable and formed in forms accessible to it for periodic review,

Desires that our imaginations be bound by the images it has abstracted

From us. The Demiurge even purchased the *Weekly* and since the takeover

Has personally overseen the advice column: *Don't be so sentimental!*

All that can be thought's been thought. All that can be felt's been felt.

Lean against the smooth stone of your countertop and feel the pristine cool.

Feel cheered you feel it; feel connected to the smooth and pristine past.

And if that's not doing it for you, go out and see a film, all listings

Are contained herein. Love culture; give its rosy cheek a kiss. Admit its

Rosy skyline's beauty. If the smog's too thick, see a film of your city's sky.

They clean that stuff up in post-. Try not to raise a fuss. Just be fucking civil.

HABEAS CORPUS

in memoriam the once-frozen North

Our collective consciousness does not allow punishment
where it cannot impose blame.

　　　　　　—*United States v. Lyons,*
　　　　　　　Judge Alvin Benjamin Rubin,
　　　　　　　dissenting

There is of course the other idea: that the intricate latticework
Of our bodies loosed from us at last will leave us free
To become anything, pure light, perhaps, or wing-beats

In fresh powder beneath some maples locked up in their thin veneer
Of ice. But then as always a sudden gust and the limbs' clacking,
And, as when some insurgent sound crosses over the porous border

Of a dream, the world recrystallizes around us: midday, snow-
Grayed, the windchill's subzero like a ball-peen to the forehead.
It's cold enough to quiet even the soul's feathery throat-song,

And so it does. Nothing moves and I move through the woods
At the edge of its city with dog, hoping he'll shit his daily shit
Before this reddening flesh numbs entirely. Nothing moves,

But beneath months-thick ice and powder, winter's put up its dead:
Squirrels and sparrows, the wren and the fox, whole families
Of field mice posed as if in the pet store's deep freeze, even,

Here and there, scattered and whole, occasional missing persons.
For now, for guilty, for guiltless, no matter, the world offers neither
Deliverance nor decay, and though we trust in that the thaw

Will come, that someday soon some pond water, water
Still and softly rippled as pre-War window-glass, will again reflect
Its image of the bloodless sky, cut, at intervals, by spring's

First returning vultures, and though the police will take then
A little comfort, as they kick the MOBILE CRIME LAB's tires
Before rolling it out for the season, that the birds help at least

To ease the legwork, we know no one's, you know, going to be
Set free. The skull's thin as eggshell so far as the beak's thick curve
Is concerned. The raisin of the eye's an easy delicacy.

And so to imagine the future is to imagine the present, but warmer,
But more forthrightly, more honestly violent. And so another day's
Bones picked clean. There is of course the idea's consolation:

For eternal patience, eternal reward, for the meek, the Earth's
Corpse. Instead, a sort of waking sleep, a sort of waking slow;
We rub our eyes, warm the last of yesterday's coffee, stare

As our email loads: surely something must have come, surely
Someone has spirited us that which would make all the difference.
We call to complain that nothing's working because we like

The on-hold music, which is a sound other than our breathing.
We ask the music if we can speak to its supervisor but when we try
To explain it only laughs, *Guiltless! Who do you think you are anyway?*,

Laughs its little soprano sax laugh before it loops back to its loop's
Beginning. The coffee pot burns mediated coal and drips acids.
The car's topped up with artillery and emits amputees. The idea was

Waking would make things clearer, would startle us as from any night's
Nightmare: these sheets' cold which is not bare concrete floor,
This patch of light the moon has cast not the interrogator's light,

This knocking in our head not some still-indecipherable code
Tapped against an adjacent wall by who knows who, by someone
We can't even begin to imagine, someone stuck here longer

Than even ourselves yet still committed to the idea that finding
A way to speak to each other might help matters, this knocking
None of that but rather something real, here, furnace clank or thief

In the night, something real and something present and not
The dream of what must be held that way until it stops thrashing,
Not the dream of being held that way, but what could be danger

Or else nothing once more, which means we prowl once more
The house, ridiculous in our underwear, ridiculous with a flashlight
Gripped like a truncheon, the floorboards cold somehow as bare

Concrete, the floorboards that croak somehow like vultures who are
Not here, who winter south, scan the Sonoran Desert's northern
Edge, its empty water bottles and tire ruts and those nameless

It dries to a sort of jerky, those nameless who labored in vain
To cross it, who had hoped that in crossing, they would be set free.
Nothing's wrong: the house secure, bolts bolted, latches latched.

Somewhere in the distance beyond the kitchen window, downtown
And its bus bench bail bondsman, downtown and its graffiti-
Covered wall's Great Writ: *Repent! The End Is Nigh! As always, as always,*

Answers the darkness. But, pre-War? In what will soon enough be
Dawn-light, in this near-light, who can tell if it's blood spread thin
On our hands or else just a healthy, living glow? Outside, the idea

Of night and the idea of day have come to a standoff.
No one's calling for negotiations. We know what happens next:
Whether the stars flicker or merely flinch, the sun, whose face

Is a badge, has always been a little trigger-happy. And though

The firestorm will consume, soon enough, everything, it seems

For the moment this will go on. As if indefinitely. As if without cause.

CIVIL TWILIGHT

> If it takes a bloodbath, let's get it over with.
> —Ronald Reagan

In this the latest version of history, which looks, as we enter into it,
Like just another block of vacants recolonized after being boarded up,
Boards now torn down but still no water or electricity and so the street

A latrine and evening's air unbroken by turned-up TV talk shows,
All the police's different voices, when they finally erupt, are so garbled
By bullhorn and two-way radio they become one and so utterly

Incomprehensible, and so the very idea of authority perfected:
Head-splittingly loud, and dumb. We walked, the sky above us fig-flesh
And flesh and baton-black at the edges, and on the bus benches and fences

Around us the Graffiti Eradication Task Force's patches of color,
Earth-toned and muted, a sort of bland abstract expressionism
Which if the world itself were art might hang on thrift store walls

Above the ten-deep stacks of Americana landscapes that sell occasionally
For frame salvage or what we might call irony if we took the time
To recognize it as such anymore, irony in the absence of perspective

Being so easily mistaken for sincerity. But who couldn't love this view's
Sudden novelty? Traffic redirected, we stood in the middle of the empty
Six-lane, stared out at the city. It was Napoleon III, when he leveled

And rebuilt Paris's poorest districts, who called them *riot-streets:*
Long, straight boulevards too wide to barricade and arranged on a grid
So that the beast of the people rising could be contained and attacked

The whole length of its body. Yet it was with no Old World stiffness,
No particular sense of occasion, only instead those peculiarly American
Virtues of efficiency and enterprise which the SWAT team,

Each individual's blood type scrawled in permanent marker upon his neck,
Descended the steel grating of their armored transport's ramp
Single file and then, in a maneuver choreographed with a textbook

Precision and punctuated by the lobbing of gas grenades,
Expanded to sweep the terrain. Mass eviction and mass arrest.
Another clearing of the land, easy as the bolt cutter's blades

Through a padlock's hardened steel, a gesture natural now after so many
Landing parties, after men on the moon. Descend and fan out
And subdue. We witnessed masters practicing the fine art

Of brutality within its legally prescribed parameters. It would be
An insult—boot tread's pressure applied with such great
Care to a bare clavicle's tender skin—to consider them

Anything less. And so like masters their labor seemed effortless, almost
Automatic, some human machinery which would not hesitate, would not
Flinch reflexively before compressing with the nightstick a stranger's

Windpipe, and which would, later on, simply crack a few
Cold ones, a day's work done. One would have to really believe,
Believe even in the face of great doubt, that helpless face, that face

Swollen by disuse; one would have to have some measure
Of faith, as, beneath his helmet of hair, Reagan, when he ordered
The bodies of students to convulse and fall, to fan out over Sproul Plaza's

Crisscrossing pavers, a cloud of CS gas pouring from the helicopters,
And guardsmen, masked and bayoneted, surrounding them, did.
It's something I hadn't thought about for a very long time: high school

Civics, our teacher's retelling of the People's Park protests in Berkeley.
I hadn't paid much attention really, eyeing, instead, in the next desk
A girl's bra strap which had strayed just outside her top's neckline,

And so which, in the dress code's terms, constituted *flagrant violation*.
I studied its lacy edge, lace's refusal to lead the eye anywhere in particular,
Its invitation to linger where one did not belong, that simple beauty

Of transgression. In May of '69, their hair down, topless young women
Offered soldiers lemonade dosed with LSD. Then beating's delirium,
Reagan's *What do you mean negotiate?*, and the dust of bulldozers undoing

Trespass, the inevitable dust of order's return. And from that hazy
Distance wasn't some moral supposed to have emerged, some parade
Of millenarians *hallelu*ing down the median-stripe, their earth-

Toned and loose-fitting clothes trembling in the breeze, their bells jangling
In exultation of that final, that most complete genocide, law,
Once and for all, having been handed down from on high? Instead,

On flesh, riot-guns inscribe their less-lethal *thou-shalt-nots*
And we're constrained from every direction: sidewalks' from-the-ground-up
Prescriptions, tattered and month-old police tape's yellowy warning

Beneath the firmament's unrelenting slate. There's something so shockingly
Ordinary about it all, its repetitiveness, how it can no longer surprise us,
Even with its sudden violence. Descend and fan out and subdue, and over

And over, until everything's tight as ship's rigging in a stiff offshore wind,
Masts and sails and rope backlit, the coast never yet fully cleared, or else
A paint-by-numbers kit's strict circumscription, where, within the lines,

Any dilettante's a master, where a small palette of colors' smoothed-out
Tones exile all detail's potential for complication. It's just so easy to take:
A benign sky, Art 101 composition which pulls the eye as if by force

Down to some singular figure just outside the background's reach.
Who is that mounted there in the distance, mesa and twilight rising
Behind him? Prince Jesus himself, maybe, lawman made manifest

And destined to occupy the whole of the territory with his gaze.
He's wearing the Gipper's hat and shifting in the Gipper's well-worn saddle
And ready to clip-clop right up to the frame's edge, to speak loudly,

To speak with one clear voice. Though of course there's nothing there
Save a stroke of cheap acrylic, a speck, a suggestion, all that was left
Of our Ronnie at the end: Great Communicator robbed of speech,

Of thought, of memory, his hair plastered in sweat across his forehead,
His soul like the Sibyl sprawled in her little jar, gasping for air.
And so his final legacy: mealtime and drug time, then bedtime for Bonzo,

The little room tidy and utterly unrecollectable, every moment another
Morning in America. To have a whole existence reduced to nothing but
Order, that invasive species in the ballast waters of history; history

Which again has its gangplank down, which storms the coast,
Which gathers those things it comes across and stores them in the hold
And forgets about them there; history which so becomes us

Without our even noticing it much, like helicopters' rattling again overhead
Or prefab bulk institutional wall art, the sort of thing that hangs
In lobbies of interstate-adjacent motels and psych-ward waiting rooms.

When I went to see you there, you leaned in and told me *all territory*
Is occupied territory, or you meant to tell me. Would have, certainly,
If you'd spoken at all. You'd never believed they'd made it to the moon—

All those hours of late-night AM talk—; you'd held out a little hope.
By the time they found your body, it had long since stopped swaying
In that small rented room off the alley, the funding for your bed long since

Slashed. I didn't hear about it for months afterward. Now, I can't
Remember much of that last time I saw you. I could hardly bear
To look, your eyes blank, what in your mind was wild, and everything else,

Subdued finally. My eyes kept wandering to that framed print behind you
As I went on about the job I'd gotten, the girl I was about
To marry. I think it was either a sunset or sunrise, something bright and

In the distance. From what I can remember, it was a very pretty picture.

DELETED SCENE

It is meant to take a while.

—Larry Levis

To forget suffering's clear drama is not truth, but cut and staged
From untold hours of tape—tape which did record, but does not now recall
How the standoff's static rage began to shift its weight from side to side,
Began, at last, to sing out boredom's favorite tunes, those lyrics'
Too-familiar complaints of this love or that longing—is to forget
The tyranny of narrative's high style. Ten-second loop, TV on mute,
The only soundtrack's the one incessant note of the stove-top exhaust fan's
Hum, and in the diffusion of its music pomegranate juice reduces,
And in well-seasoned carbon-steel, duck breasts render skin-side-down,
And standing over them there, a man half-watches the screen as somewhere's
Barricades razor up in darkness. There are police, riot-geared, and then—
The picture crisper than the world itself—gas canisters' first arcing volleys,
Stun guns' first incapacitating jolts. Tegucigalpa or Tehran, some post-
Cold-War-Nowhere-istan? The anchors have already moved on.
Because the people fell so easily—seemed so fully living and then suddenly
Nothing more than that unconjugated abandonment of *to fall*—

He would want to say they must be somewhere already under a tremendous

Weight, not Earth itself's dead center, sure, but certainly some other place

Both hot and poor. *Would want to say,* I said, except that gravity,

He knows, is one of our few laws that applies its force everywhere

And without discrimination. It is ruthless; he knows this,

And so, in the final appraisal, those limp figures' motion says nothing

Of *where* or *who* or *why;* is worthless except to illustrate that

For which there's already no demand: the *what*'s never-ending proof

Of basic principles. So for the carcass's damp *thunk*

When he slid it into the trash, *the weight of a thing is what pulls it down;*

And for the ease with which he coaxed the muscle's membrane

From the bone, *the body can offer only a little resistance,* and so now

For this flare-up's mist, for its aerosolized cayenne and garlic, its heat

In his eyes and constriction of his lungs, bronchioles narrowing near

To the panic which necessarily must accompany so many nerves firing

In unison, firing at full force, so much strong, so much unexpected

Feeling, Brute Fact taunts: *Dear Consciousness? Poor Soul?*

Whatever it is you think you are is hardly there at all! You're involuntary,

A little blood muscled through ductwork, which, when it pools in the brain

And is later played back to you as a neuroimager's Rorschach rendition

Reminds you of absolutely nothing so much as the distant, indistinct flowering

Of a carpet-bombing's declassified satellite footage. You're the stupid truth:

When everything's gonna burn, you can't tell a story but the story of fire.

And maybe if he'd have heard it over the kitchen's thrumming drone,

And maybe if he weren't just now gathering his bearings—the countertop

Tile cool, the TV crystalline, and a little rain out the window streaking

The streetlight like the static we'll never see again—he'd want to allow

It could be right. What other answers could we hope for? What's possibility

Hasn't already been measured, been quantified and so accounted for,

Been coded and consigned to those vast architectures of the Depository

Of What Is and What Therefore Must Be's server cloud? Who could resist

That world without guesswork, with no flicker of doubt,

With no Zapruder film's juke and stagger as the motorcade seems first

And almost imperceptibly to pause and is then suddenly swarmed

By black-suited and no-longer-secret police? And the people

Who'd been the crowd? They're no longer a crowd at all

But again only people, and people running every which way now,

Running for dear life, the tattered hems of their garments

Brushing the faces of the trampled, the air choked with leaded

Gas's over-rich mixture, and the world then never the same.

Or else the world, for a moment, more brightly what it had been all along:

Another retina-searing testament to itself on a roadside LED billboard,

Where, Lord, every color's revelation, every form the Absolute's

Manifestation. There is just this world you see, just the matter of its fact.

Grease spatter. Synaptic patter. First there's the moment of cognition,

Then recognition, that unmovable weight of all we've known:

You may come this close, it tells us, *no closer. There are rules.* And so

In the basement of the Bureau of Each and Every Last Contingency,

The staffers huddled in the Situation Room cheer—after all their research's

Tediousness, the failed trials, the double-blind control—the fulfillment

Of their leather-folioed fantasies, people having come at last

To resemble so closely animals cowering in submission, which of course

Has always been—according to the data, the white papers, the plasticine

Models of the central nervous system—their proper classification.

It's a story of the triumph of science. Who could do anything

But suspend disbelief? And never mind if even high definition's

Millions of pixels per frame don't allow a viewer to perceive directly

Such minutiae, such peripheral concerns to the story at hand.

We must trust in the knowledge that, as matters which have been subjected

To the rigors of study and of form, these are settled affairs. And so

With the science of stories, a field which, understanding the importance

Of paying its debts, ends by making all its formulas available to us.

If on a hot day you stare long enough, you can almost see them

Hemming in the distance, almost hear them inside your head then,

Skreaking out the Emergency Broadcast System's shrill test-tone

In your fillings. For the greater good, the public trust. For the airwaves

All aquiver with broadband broadcast's glistering wavelengths.

Because there is nowhere else to move, we move in them and they

In us, and each utterly indifferent to the other, indifferent

To the story this tells, which is neither the story of those people there

Nor of we people here, nor any people anywhere, but is the story

Of watching apart from the story of what's watched, the story's

Telling apart from the story of what's told, the story of how seeing

Hardened until it became a way of believing, a story which turned first

To bone and then to rock and then, like the fossil record itself, dead, buried,

Becomes the story of that to which we are so happily indifferent. It is

Without question; is story, arrested. And there beside it in the street,

Knees bloodied by gravel and wrists bound in Zip Ties behind its back,

Arms and face all welts and divots, is Hope Itself's Last, Best Hope:

To be able to imagine anything else. Which means not only the coming

Airstrike as something other than inevitable, but even the airstrike,

As it arrives, not soundtracked, not choreographed, not peppered

With screen-tested one-liners and somehow leading up to Tom Cruise

And Goose hamming it up at the piano, or later, Goose dead in the water,

Our tears so precisely jerked, the blood in the sea not disappearing

As some token or sign of its final and utter insignificance

But thanks to the people in Special Effects slicking up instead, like oil.

It coats everything. Its sheen obscures even the thing itself, reflects back

Blacked-out sky shot with iridescence, refracts the whole lost history

Of life on this planet compressed until it becomes again

That only thing we know how to look for: fuel for fire, for forge,

The broad blades that dig pits and the fine blades that chip stone,

For machines that haul rebar, that pour the great concrete walls

Of county courthouses, Chambers of Commerce, and the state prisons

Around which congregate new mini-malls, new golf courses, new realtors'

And insurance agents' kids' finger-paintings tacked on cubicle walls.

For the taming of a desolate countryside. For the warden's early tee time,

The luxury of his mulligan, his practice swing, his Rolex's stoic tick

And his yellow silicone bracelet's silence even as it fights for the cure.

For time for leisure. For time to breathe the air, to measure the fairway

With one's gaze, to chug a beer before work and for the edge off, then,

The necessity of doing what must be done. So noted. So notarized.

So sealed and archived and so now the chemicals arranged according

To their purpose in the infinite division of labor's infinite division of guilt:

To only swab the skin sterile. To merely excite the vein. To latch

The door, draw the blinds, to wait for the signal. So for the death-

Chamber's cold tile, its tile layer, for Velcro wrist restraints' strength,

Lost moments, and for the time to choose a few words, for the time,

For once, to have one's words listened to, written down, for choosing

Go fuck yourselves, and for the ingenious fashioning of Velcro's tiny barbs,

For ingenuity, the machines that build the machines that dig pits,

Tamp earth, and lay sod over the blood of a landscape ready

For the Dairy Council's next *Healthy & Happy* ad blitz. Heart-flutter?

Piston-sputter? Who could think of such things for long? Who could resist

The director's triumphant *that's a wrap!,* mission accomplished,

Then the after-party's laughter, the open bar's endless kamikazes,

The cake artist's vision of frosting and fondant reminiscent

Of a jet engine's stylized flame? Who could refuse it? Who could

Become anything but what is unattainable in refusal's necessary

And unattained precondition: take nothing as granted. Rates

Of airborne dispersal, diplomatic plates, bulletproof glass, the little story

He was planning to tell you over dinner. And remember

That on the dead beach, the pelican drenched in crude and not yet dead,

No matter how statuesque she looks, no matter how bronzed,

Was not posing for the photographer, not loving the attention, not hoping

To make the cover, which, because of its exquisite design,

Its immaculate framing, seems both natural and necessary

To the composition of this stack of unsorted mail. Who could

Attend to it all? The six threads of saffron, the pinch of salt,

The vastness of that which we cannot bring ourselves to face?

Who could not file them away and cease to think them further,

These equations by which our lives are figured? For pinot with the duck,

The dance we make of falling. For what is fruit-forward, what is lush,

Asphalt on the back of the tongue. And for the vested interest?

What could refute it? If not an indistinct head's tilt back

And to the left, not a set of x coordinates, not a set of y,

And not staring again, staring endlessly, at a fiftieth-generation copy

Of a VHS Handycam's frame-by-frame while hoping still

To see the grand scheme of things flash momentarily across the screen

Like a salvation. It won't. And if anyone at all is going to show,

Is going to give some definitive form to that analog distortion's

Obsolescence, give some order to that undifferentiated dark,

You know as well as I, it's going to be the cops. And so before

The helicopters zero in on the heat signatures of our bodies

And the whole neighborhood's peeking from the corners

Of their front windows, there's something I want to say to you;

I just don't know how. But if we had the time to sit with each other,

Eat, if we had time to fill ourselves and the time, together, to dream,

Then—off the record, no photos—I'd like to imagine the moment

We could imagine a moment when the disfigured world did not

Fold back again on itself and into a history which was already its future.

That would be something, at least. Something more than desire's

Impossibility, or the way Beauty kicks Suffering in the shin,

Tells it to stand up, keep walking, because the Promised Land,

It keeps saying, is just over the next rise. And even though by now

Both know there's nothing there but another tract of desert, land-mined,

Mortar-pocked, I can't figure what to have them do but walk. What

Wouldn't ruin the pacing or compromise the delicate balance of the plot's

Thematic unity? What could ever test well enough to make the final cut?—

Which anyway is ready now to print, and which, as you'll have no doubt

Imagined, was never able to find a way out of itself but this one,

The only way that feels right, feels satisfying: a splash of acid

To balance the richness, the shimmer of fat about to burn in the pan.

OFFERING OF
TWO BURNING CALVES

The other kind, I mean, and also the thighs; and up from the blacktop's
Blistering of potholes, its bitumen-stench, heat quarries out this thin sole-
Rubber's insulation, quarries out of muscle all that which was not already
Pain, and out of day's light itself the crisp definition which once granted us
Something that could still pass for a vision, as if undistorted, of this world,
Something that didn't always make perfect sense, but looked good enough
In passing, and so mostly avoided begging the question. No longer.
Not in the face of this sky set finally to make good on its threat to melt,
To drip down and pool on the wiry afternoon's horizon. And sure,
It would be fair, at this point, to demand some answers—about, for one,
The supposed necessity of misery's necessity, or the long-promised right
Of carrying the water of the wrong—, but as uncertainties compound,
Explanations volatilize. Attempts whither. It's perfectly natural to protest,
To beg the least bit of clarity, that rarest of elements, or some sense
How life came suddenly to resemble little but its own rust-streaked slag heap,
But prayers, we must by now have learned, are answered unevenly, at best,
Which means that although this pain we've been given can be safely counted
Among the most readily available means for those who hope to find focus,

One dignity it will never allow us is that of a say in things: the object
To which it binds our unflinchingly flinching attention is always its own.
And so now the nothing-else-ness of this single detail—what couldn't possibly
Amount to more than the subtlest shading, an equation hardly worth figuring,
In the back of the County Surveyor's dimmed but precisely plotted
Imagination—: a road's slight upward grade at an intersection.
To recognize it at all is to find oneself bent amidst failure:
Radiator blown or engine dead or else the transmission's planetary gears
Ground down and seized, their intricate turnings shredded upon the idea
Against which we so long ago leveraged our very selves: the enduring value
Of freedom, its promise that we might go where we like, do as we wish.
It's an idea that, if we could neglect to take it, for a moment, at its word—
That, for instance, all those direct debits to the First Integrated Bank
Of the Realized Body & Soul have been invested wisely and will yield
Great dividends—we would see only shards of which remain anymore,
Just so much shattered safety-glass, or another bottle hurled against the curb
In what we might call despair if we'd dare grant all these stumbling drunks
The dignity of emotionally complex inner lives. Or life at all beyond
A wandering off to the nowhere in particular that lies everywhere outside
Our immediate field of vision. *Dear Child,* we were told, *you must work
To make of the future that which you choose.* Those who suffer suffer
Only the consequences. But after a while, even our most solidly built delusions
Can't help but give up to repetitive stress's eventual fatigue and fracture,
That going-nowhere's endless motion which now neither we nor it
Can say was ever good for anything other than its own perpetuation.
And what are we supposed to do, when we still owe so much on this?
Choice long ago succumbed to its planned obsolescence, but the Laboratories
Of Defeat have thankfully created for us endless variations of a still-possible
Experience, and this iteration, since it must answer the no-longer-adorned

Contempt—chorus of curse, horn, The Finger, fists striking steering wheels—

That the orderly world pours down on us when we're revealed as anything less

Than perfect order, is to throw the thing in neutral, door swung wide

Into the adjacent lane, and to push. It is to offer up, again, everything.

And even if only for nothing. And even if only for the irrevocable judgment

Of NEWS 7's hovering Eye in the Sky: —lane two—disabled vehicle—unfit

    for the road—.

On-screen, wide-angled backups measure the miles. To push,

And to be defeated, even in that. It must all have the look

Of prophecy: from the triumphs of industry, the downfall of the industrious—.

Or something like that. Whatever works for ratings. Whatever gives

Some little comfort that when the rubble of the day-to-day's unsaleable tragedy

Is finally settled and accounted for, something else—what might pass,

Even, as a way to live—might be salvaged. But until then, what—abandoned

To the still-churning smoke of cities, the elemental force of friction's burn—

Comes of the newly pariahed? It's easy to imagine, from this prophetic

Distance, that there must be at least a little consolation in some time to oneself,

Time to think as one wants or go where one likes or do as one might wish,

But when someone's classic rock radio blares Janis's *freedom's just another word*

For nothing left to lose, you'll understand now why you've always hated that song:

The impossible romance of its bargain. There's the VIN on the dash

And the VIN stamped into the engine block. Fingerprints are everywhere.

Here, you say, *just take it all.* Really though, what would you have it do but balk?

You, dumb arms outstretched, your hands cupped around your FICO score,

Your social, your name; your hands holding for it what is already its own.

SORT OF LIKE, UM, THE FALCON & THE FALCONER OR WHATEVER, BUT SORT OF NOT

Therefore hell hath enlarged herself, and opened her mouth
without measure.

—Isaiah 5:14

Consider now how great must be that whole
which unto such a part conforms itself.

—Dante

Surely *some* revelation is at hand—

—Yeats (emphasis added)

Where at last the livestock exhibition's halogen-stilled interior opens
Upon the midway's dieseled-in dizziness, the merry-go-round's incessant
Over and again, what, the self-service hand sanitizer stations ask us,
Could we possibly be besides that which must be cleansed?
And cleansed, and at ease, the ethanol goo having left as artifact
Of its own evaporation a pristine coolness, what are we now but the need

To be warmed, filled by batters fried and sugared and stuck with skewers,

Their scents spiced by the nearby sows' pissed-in hay, the rabbits' salt licks?

It's a thing a person might like to say a thing about, those scents' mingling,

A thing to put a point on at least as fine as the pygmy goat's sculpted horn,

Something about a meaning somewhere inhering in it, some nourishing

Commonplace, some sweetness and sour as if kneeled and pleading

For its own revelation. And isn't that, after all, how one writes a poem

Or manages, this morning just as the last, to get up again, to keep going,

Not really in spite of everything, but rather without spite for anything?

Life is beautiful. So too the world. And one must only accept it as it is

To be taken into its good grace, be offered, for instance, this idea of Truth

As a grease stain's memory of what must, looking back, seem satisfaction:

Blood bathing in warmth a stomach full of the nearly indigestible,

The body's center of gravity suddenly lower, nearer the Earth,

Leaden, so nearer too in spirit to these almost unidentifiable remains

Of a harvest festival's promise: that we might escape our work, want,

And so, by extension, everything that's become recognizable

As the self. Maybe you'd like to imagine women somewhere to illustrate it,

Aprons thrown off like fetters, cupboards stocked for winter with jams which,

Before they were closed away from light, were radiant as we all desire to be.

O, to be desire and not want, be abandoned to each other in a festival's crowd,

Be autumn air's seducing teeth and abandonment congregated

Until it finds its own rhythm, its own drink and dance. And go ahead—

Who would stop you?—because to imagine such a thing would be good

As any silence or carnival music's mechanized piping, would be its own void,

Its own ceding of ability to speak at all about, for instance, the sanction

Of a hell's perceptual architecture, its order no folktale's anarchy,

But merely an image of one as conceived in the collective consciousness

Of a Limited Liability Corporation, its subcontractors and consultants,

Its affiliate entities, an image dictated by the terms of its own licensure:

Zoning regs and noise ordinances, health code, the institutional structure

Of local and state centers of power, their Blue Ribbon Commissions.

Which are an invocation of silence. Are silence repeating its own name

And gaveling itself to order until it becomes lightheaded, short of breath,

Disoriented or high or convinced of the reality of its own being

To such a degree now that when it finds itself among others it sees nothing

But its own reflection, which it finds entrancing: the meaningful gaze

That meaninglessness returns to us. And how our staring at it fills time,

Becomes our name enthralled of itself, outside itself, until even its face,

After a while, seems just one more object, not really anyone's at all,

But a comfort in the way it's familiar, the way it rises each morning

Without spite, the way it goes on, even as it craves something beyond itself.

After living like this a long time, it finally finds the nerve to ask for a date,

And so now, hand in hand, amidst what we can only call a frenzy

Of light and buzzing and beasts with all the last roughness bred out—

And with these words out suddenly those beasts' very meaning

Reveals itself in our admiration: a coxcomb's variegations

Testify that we must be what clicks, what whispers to them

That, no matter what the judge might mark on his clipboard,

No matter how little say they've had in what's become of them,

They're still very pretty birdies—, now what could we possibly be

But this willingness to pony up, to pay the going price

For the privilege of being what's whirled by meth-mouthed transients

In the Gravitron's, the Super Swing's, the Tilt-A-Whirl's relentless circles?

And we will empty the air from our lungs. Will be testament that the cry

Can go on even after the sound has gone out, which must mean

This must be life, this feeling like something substantial pressing outward

From within us, this feeling so necessary to nurturing the specter

Of that other promise: something, Great God, something's gonna come.

A rooster scritches at its feed. Some kid from the FFA does not feel horror

As he sells his prize hog. And under the Civic Center's resentfully low

Ceilings, their windowless, timeless light, the Department of Eschatology's

Preliminary Hearings—unfortunate formality—are open to Public Comment,

The Draft Environmental Impact Report having finally been read

In full. And so this morning I stood and straightened my tie

Or smoothed the line of my skirt, expressed my honest gratitude

For being allowed to say a few words, to inquire after a few concerns.

It's always strange to speak before others, but most especially the powerful,

To speak while they sip infinitely clear water from infinitely clear glass,

While they adjust their gaze through this portion, then that of their bifocals.

They move through ancient turns of the head to sharpen their chins'

Shadows and glacial cycles of the wrist to check boxes on forms.

Turns out you can go on babbling forever, go on pleading for answers.

No one cares. The inevitable—they smudge the corners of their eyes—

Is still the inevitable. There's only the matter of getting round to it,

Of tiring, and in doing so, affirming that most insidious oath of loyalty:

I have no further questions. And isn't that, anyway, how one goes on

Writing poems? Look long enough, and the world will offer itself up,

Right in front of the eyes, so that we can say it was a lovely morning

To rise to, and that this is a lovely evening to be out. I'm so glad

I finally asked you. And never mind about my day—what a bore I can be!

Tell me about yourself, about the way your path through life came clear

And proved positive, proved beyond any doubt that we are more

Than some great lapse of memory or half-amusing sideshow

That drags on as the Spiritus Mundi sifts endlessly through the sands,

Torturing and burning those things it finds there. Tell me about being

At ease, about what it's like to loose oneself upon the world, lose this worry,

And just count up our tickets, get in line for a spin, and be at ease

With what tethers us, which would be to know the exact length of a law

So tightly bound that need of anything but that which has been met

Can no longer be conceived. What joy! To know no answer

But the right-in-front-of-us. And which holds. Always holds.

RESOLUTION IN LOVING MEMORY OF SKY & GOOSEFLESH

With their feet deep in the dust of the earth as desolate as the sky, they went along with the resigned look of men who are condemned to hope forever.

—Baudelaire

The air may be thin, but it is what can be breathed.

—Robert Hullot-Kentor

"Hope" is the thing with feathers—

—Dickinson

Having begun now to burn bright as the fires that bore it, having,

As so many things, become of what it was from the first the apparent

Equal, transformed only through atomization, through display,

Those distinctive signatures of the miraculous and its window dressers'

Ongoing project—Design's gentrification of a vulgar, impoverished Real—,

Which, on-schedule, over-budget, will spare not one of us its curatorial

Light and the touch, feathered at the edges, of its sentimental reflections,

We've been called here today by these contrails' inscrutable skywriting,

By their invocation of that charred, nameless chasm, that scorched no-

Man's-land that separates a pictographic glyph's gape-mouthed gawk

At *that thing right there* from the disinterested, abstract yawn any alphabet

Would offer in return for such a gauche archaism, called here to gather

In memory of what by the end of this will have already been forgotten.

Let us therefore resolve again *never again,* and make of our bodies the shape

Of hope as it's portrayed in the artist's conception of its future reenactment,

A shape the contours of which—and this is hardly avoidable, the poverty

Of concrete possibilities having narrowed down to what, only a few years ago,

Would have seemed like unimaginably austere notions of necessity—

Take something first of Officialdom's and then of the prime-time procedural's

Form, and we mention this now, I should mention, if for no other reason

Than to at least begin to account for what will strike us all as a heightened

Police presence, but which, in reality, is nothing out of the ordinary, the sky

No longer there to provide us anything other than police helicopters' circling,

And finally because we have become one with our God, it takes also the form

Of God, which is content, and the true content of God the form of giving in.

Whereas the sky was the vault of heaven, and thereby held God at bay.

Whereas I was intent on the form of her thigh and how the sky sometimes
With a cold pulled taut the everyday until you began to notice it all over
Again, although what we called it called to mind already a carcass, plucked.

Whereas the form of God is what stifles and is not spaciousness, not space.

Whereas intent on nothing but not waking, I sometimes dream a memory

Like cold, or like the stories we were told about freezing to death,

And how, in the end, it's supposed to be a sort of calm, how it's supposedly

Not so bad, though even its dream can never keep the day from coming,

The day that only ever half-arrives but does so all at once: brittle, thin,

Impenetrable, finally, as what now fills what was once the sky,

Our Dear Departed Friend, our friend who grew ill, who grew, in illness,

Less and less recognizable, so that when we thought, as we occasionally would,

To keep the sky in our hearts during the hardly bearable middle of a day,

It was something almost entirely different that filled them then, something

Vague and near, something no longer what could be watched from a distance.

Whereas there is a point at which the sick give up or give in to it,

Can no longer stand the ache of it, or sweat's constant beading, a point

At which illness overtakes a thing, so that what comes to fill it is not it

But only that which has metastasized, stiffened, swelled to the bursting point,

And then, burst finally, is only the shape of what's lost become decay itself,

An atmosphere hard and lustrous suddenly as anthracite and smoldering

In the traditional if not somewhat ostentatious style of the coal seam fire

That once some perpetually terrified and already near-dead ancestor of ours

Saw crack the Earth and breath sulfur at the very moment he first dreamt hell.

Whereas these our Beloved have been called back to that Realm of Pure Form

Scrubbed of Content, that infinite's semblance which, in bad lighting, begins

To look like pure delusion, we rejoice now in this deliberate light that guides us

Not to brood on might-have-beens, not second-guess doctors' orders or search

Our charts, as if we could even get our hands on them, for a wrong

At which to focus our anger and thereby make it righteous—a preventative care

Withheld or, as measured against the state-of-the-art's peer-reviewed best,

Some malpractice—, this light that guides us rather to accept explanation's

Inaccessibility, it having been sealed in behind the backlit, abraded glass walls

Of a private room in the hospital's exclusive new luxury wing, its design

An elaborate overlaying of suffering's sleep with a feathery glow while outside

And in the distance some smoke or dust plume rises, reminds us by its way

Of signaling the end of some something we took for granted that, realistically,

We have to assume all our records' arcane scrawl has been by now modulated,

Digitally, and in a process subject too to both the Official Secrets Act

And HIPAA compliance, two of a class of sacred texts, neither written by man

Nor able to be read with any comprehension of their real-world implications,

Which, collectively, are known for nothing but the cross-armed refusal

They maintain in the face of any questions, transposed into disembodied

Ever-presentness, a sort of threat as the threat of its own materialization,

That moment when, in the one version of history we feel must be somehow

Inevitable, our name is pulled up on a dash-mounted display somewhere

So that the squad car and the cars from the Bureau of Health that accompany it,

And also so that the men inside the cars, men themselves so sure of themselves,

Might finally, and as if from nowhere, fulfill their collective destiny

Of appearing as the flourish of their own authority, an occasion commemorated

By the carving of authority's initials' meaningless meaning first into our flesh

And then across the worn cover of our permanent record's last extant hard copy

Right before someone throws its corporeal husk to the fire or paper shredder,

The scanning and encryption of its apotheosis done and over with.

Whereas the thigh was the vault of heaven and thereby kept death at bay,

Or anyway the sense of it, the sound of its reminder alarms, the rustling arrival

Of its Second and later its Final Notices, kept it at bay long enough sometimes

You could live, and with a childlike disregard for, among the other things,

The persistent inconclusiveness of our test results, and even that place

The future has made for us, that place once far off and what could be watched

From a distance, what was yet to be filled in, but which, when you shift

In its direction now is a hot wind from some desert you've never imagined,

Some place God appeared once to men, appeared and spoke in soothing tones

Just before he firebombed them and then in his diary wrote it all out

In a distracted, distant voice that came to find official form in law.

Whereas what was once distant and like a space between all of this

And something else was so where hope seemed most like something palpable,

Something that needed to be nurtured by staring off into that distance

And staring too at the closest things and believing, after every reasonable

Objection, it all deserved care, that all of it—because as much as we were

It too was in fact there—deserved to be taken care of, to be taken in,

Be fed if hungry and given some way to live and become whatever

It might of its own accord become, a sense sometimes the sky would punctuate

By letting fall near sidewalks or beneath bushes nestlings, fledglings,

Helpless little details—pinfeather and open mouth, eyes not really eyes

But pupils only—, details so out of step with the purpose and intent

Of those our long morning marches to school they went almost

Unnoticed, except that though the young know already to dread the march,

They do not yet know it is sinful to let dread slow our pace and show us,

In slowness, each detail we will with great effort have to learn not to see,

Not to lose a few valuable moments with, the sky still a far-off thing

That did not yet press in on us and confine us so completely in ourselves.

Whereas our grief's formed in the remembrance to which it's been pressed,

I remember we'd kneel down to the sidewalk's morning dampness, a memory

Of something clean or else a clean and never-put-to-some-other-purpose

Memory—dampness, and cold—and in our hands hold the ghost of a sparrow

Or wren or mockingbird or jay that neither we nor it recognized as a ghost,

It still seeming to be in its own body and not just a memory of itself, kneel

And cup them in our palms and walk them with us to school, to class,

And then for the whole of the day pay to whatever it was we were meant

To pay it—long division's insoluble and mute remainders, maybe,

Things that the industrious among us, some latter-day class reunion's

Actuaries and securities brokers and midlevel meth distributors,

Had already begun to understand as an ur-form of profit, what could be

Skimmed and pocketed while a show was made of evening things up,

Or, later, during another afternoon's slow and slowing constriction,

Reading comprehension, and in that endeavor all our test results'

Inconclusiveness, a state which was, because though we could well enough

Repeat back what things had said, somehow we still wanted more,

Persistent—we'd pay it no attention at all while in the classroom's far corner,

Confined in some box that could on short notice pass reasonably

For shelter, what we'd not yet learned not to care for, what we'd not yet learned

Must be consigned to natural causes' brutality shivered terribly and unnoticed.

Whereas when, by next morning, these birds, just babies, we'd think, were dead

Or else died cupped in our palms as we without effect pled for them

To drink from an eyedropper or eat something from the tip of a toothpick,

We had no way of knowing we'd let them slip into hypothermia's slow fade,

Which is of course archaic now with its ridiculous childhood memory of cold

As a sort of cleanliness, its idea that there's a way to go other than the worst.

Whereas the bullies would later become police or street-level dealers
And would for the future's whole choked remainder find each other
Along sidewalks or behind bushes, faces pressed to drain grates, eye only pupil,
Blood pressure only spike, the blacktop retaining day's heat through night
And then offering it back to day again, intense and reliable as our profession
Of belief in our affirmation that the children are our future, which affirms,
In fact, our capacity to forget those children in the present already chewed
By the past, only messes of them left now baking on the asphalt.

Whereas it was under the auspices of an unknown agency that we filled

With what the world made ready for us, accepted already as children

Even those days at recess as conforming to the contours of a deadly math,

A logic God himself first employed when in retrospect we decided only he

Might judge the proper rate of exchange for innocents lost to promise renewed:

When a storm surge overtook the sandbox, always someone ready to choose,

To direct the dead and dying to be correct in both number and arrangement,

To orchestrate and account for the enactment of choking and flailing below,

Those lucky few who'd managed to scramble, slamming others aside,

To the top of the slide's high ground, its wealthy vantage point,

Surviving to bear witness's burden, to bear the responsibility of going on,

Of rebuilding, with its way of obscuring those lost behind the scaffolding

Of our nicest niceties, of a *we'll get through this* repeated often enough to nourish

That blunt something already pulsing, swelling at the brain stem's base and now

About to sprout: the redeveloper's reptile imagination, its meager bloom.

Whereas the city destroyed is a pure form, the land blank but pre-parceled,

The idea of suffering's emptiness become reality, a despair that finds

Expression in the shocked-open mouth's loss of speech, loss of sound,

While yet every tendon strains, seemingly intent on fighting, forcing

Its way through the skin and then beyond the body's bounds entirely,

As if the things that link us together could not, at last, stand even to be in us.

Whereas what I wanted to say is that that's what it's begun to feel like,
   physically,
Inside of me: somehow baby birds, necks lifted, beaks open, and not a breath-
Sound even, not a gasp, only the silence of absolute need's vacuum,
A sort of hissing distance after that moment when there is suddenly no longer
Such a thing as distance and so no longer such a thing as any other place to go,
The ribcage's vaulted design stressed by heat and pressure in excess of its
   rating.

So be it resolved that therein lie promise's nearly imperceptible remains:

The shape with nothing of it left inside and the ache, then, for anything,

Anything at all to rush in, fill it, swell it with some meaning, even if only that

Of an angry God's tantrum, or this dust-storm God, in jealousy, kicked up

Over our advances in the fields of design, of thermodynamics, actuarial science,

And all those banalities of remote control and digital imaging that would, once,

Have been worthy of burnt calves or whatever other sacrifice that, petulantly,

The miraculous seemed to demand in exchange, when even exchange—

For death, knowledge, for fire's industriousness, eternal torment—was miracle

And not merely another banality, a few dollars slipped to the cashier

Beneath the bulletproof glass's barrier for Cheetos and somewhere

Whole regions swallowed up in a darkness forgotten by the next news cycle,

Its prophetically tinged annunciations, which in the heat wave have become

Tiresome as everything else, so you switch to the next station, which offers,

In exchange for not thinking about it, the sort of blunt statements of fact

That start to sound like perfectly good explanations: *hot town summer in the city.*

In witness whereof on this Day of Our Lord our God will be a stupid one,

And mean, will be stupid meanness deified in direct proportion to the severity

Of our drought, our death toll, our official language, will be God in the form

Of anger, of blunt air, blunt water, blunt earth, a God versed in the style

Of vivisection's laying bare of things—*blood still pumping there, and look!*

This sinuous thing here's rhythmic tensing—, a style that demonstrates

How knowledge's yield, as so many things, multiplies beyond belief

When cultivated with additions of bloodmeal, bonemeal, steam rising

From carcasses already begun to decay in the rendering plant's yard

While inside the board members assure, signing their checks to the Senator's

Reelection Committee, that the pathogen comes from anywhere but here,

They being men in the image of a God who dissembles as we're disassembled.

Be it resolved that the very moment of mentioning malpractice entails also

This other one, which is a disclaimer, and unsays everything I've said,

The form of which has been plausible denial, the content lies of omission,

Because the idea of a truth, in order to survive, must become a negotiable

Instrument, a promissory note singed around the edges and collateralized

Against pure delusion's unending ability to find the bright side, to imagine

A situation wherein mass death can be written off as a cost of doing business,

The profit of which is a certainty that, from some perspective, this must all

Be a sort of necessity, a dark but inescapable moment in a limitless promise's

Eventual fulfillment, so so be it if this sand's wind-whipped signature

Must etch itself across the covers of the library's whole collection,

Even the dull, one-color ones of the ethics and climatology journals,

Which, in the end, neither we nor the wind even bothered to read—

Their resubscription cards buried in stiff, still-unbroken bindings—

Before they became among the first things we threw hastily atop the new city

Wall's makeshift, and which like all things subjected to peer review's

Institutionalized rigor, stand zero chance of helping in this case or any other.

In witness whereof God's long-form birth certificate is tattooed in cuneiform

On the eyewall of the hurricane and the rising tide's inside-bottom lip,

And in that strict sense can be said to have been released to the public.

Be it resolved further, and farther, and faster still until nothing is left of it

Save Officialdom's disdain for what cannot be made to conform: the thigh,

For one, how once the cold pulled taut its skin over muscle, bone, marrow,

Pulled taut the contours of what, at the time, seemed the only thing,

And so what, at the time, had a sort of power beyond the reach of edicts

Issued once by some slumped cleric or hapless Pope and later too

By such beacons of humanity, such shining cities on such shining hills,

Men whose luster blots out the yet-redeveloped lusterlessness of the slums below

That they'd ne'er deign set foot in, men as Messrs. Pat Robertson

And Joseph McCarthy, who hated it for what it knew and would not tell them:

The very shape of their Kingdom come—sterile paradise—mirror-imaged

And in the negative and right there for them to see if they would only learn

To love something beyond a self's desire to destroy the not-it, that distance

Beyond which it's become increasingly impossible to see, the horizon pressed

Close-in, the air exhausted of its own red-flag warnings, and the UV

Having scorched our retinae, which have at this point become so brittle

We can hardly turn our head without them sparking against our skulls,

A risk too great to take when the danger of brush fires is so severe.

In witness whereof in the end it was not men, but a mobilization

Of the various contractual entities which had absorbed them and found form,

Fully realized, in industry's endlessly repetitive capacity for innovation,

A thing that, as we were told in school, brings us closer, makes the world

A smaller place, which is why we have now gathered to preach in this in-fill's

Sprawling midst, perched here ridiculously on a street corner at the dead center

Of nothing at all and atop an apple crate which may have never existed

And certainly hasn't existed for a very long time except in the stock footage

That's been sold to us: imagination's mass-produced stand-in, inescapable

As the sound of passing traffic or, overhead, a flight path's fiery roar

And the toxic specter fire haunts us with, its dioxins and dioxides

That rain down and rise up both, saturate and solidify what was once the sky

And is now its own burial shroud, a thing, yes, that conceals, yet at long last,

Has no sense of decency, has, rather, a papal aptitude for the enforcement

Of shame's shamefulness, a sense that, now that we're packed into such close

Quarters, such stifled space, amounts mostly to a nearness without touch

And the fear of bringing a child into such a world, a fear that, in light

Of the technology of shame's stunning advancements, from the fig leaf first

To the burqa to finally this hazmat suit's absolutely unassailable modesty—

How even in the decontamination shower's humiliation it reveals nothing,

How its outer shell's trademarked, patent-pending synthetic is impermeable

To even temptation, the vague sensations it does admit stirring a shudder at

Rather than a memory of touch—a fear that probably needn't concern us much,

And which anyway, like the now-familiar sound of infants or toddlers

Sniveling in a not-too-distant somewhere, is probably something

We'll build up a reasonable tolerance for, we being endlessly adaptable things.

Be it resolved that the UV we will tell ourselves splashes lightly across our face

Splashes in fact like bleach and that it, along with heat itself, will prove

Not only the most cost-effective, but indeed the most readily available methods

Of sterilization, methods against which even the thigh, though eminently

Decent, had no defense, and so left us stranded thereby in the middle of a life

Concerned primarily with the proper filling and filing of petitions,

Our arms full with sheaves of paper—marriage certificates, birth

And death certificates, evidence of cohabitation's joint checking accounts

And utility bills—, our nostalgia for the little sentimentalities we once allowed

Ourselves as our name slipped through the mail slot, pre-printed and joined up

With some other one, sentimentalities the potential of which is only realized

When their transfiguration as proof of eligibility is completed, coded, filed,

And this will certainly be any day now, you just have to learn to wait,

The line snaking as it does around the concrete courtyard of some low building,

Our documents clutched tight against the firestorm's nearly irresistible updraft

While you dream of a voucher's worth of meltwater and a ration of something

Besides this to feel: the ache in the arch of our feet and in everything the ache.

In witness whereof I would tell you it is wrong for anyone, at the last moment,

To have to feel terror, except that both moral claims and the subjunctive lie

Desiccated in the ashen, cracked remains of a language no longer able

To support them, no longer able to accommodate, syntactically or otherwise,

Even their pleas, which at any rate no one takes so seriously anymore,

Their refusal to contract a reputable third-party accreditation agency's

Systematized scrutiny having become, quite frankly, a little embarrassing,

As if we were to take it as an article of faith that what cannot be said

Just once and brutally, or cannot be fit formulaically around an equals sign,

Is not necessarily out to pull one over on us, to blind us to the fact that it is

Perhaps no more consequential than a feathery corpse interred in a shoebox

And buried someplace meant to be forgotten, and anyway surely by now rotted

And so unmistakably subject—don't make him say it again—to God's anger,

Which is unequivocal and can be spoken only in short, staccato sentences

Any idiot could understand, or if not understand in any substantial sense

At least feel the immediate terror of, every idiot and everyone else too

Being versed in the style of the brutal, the way it, without any embarrassment,

Makes the case for itself by excluding the case for anything else, the fact,

Namely, that in the future all our death will be close quarters, hot,

Will call our name from the roll and make us step toward it and mark us

Present, our pupil widening uncontrollably and light bruising our retina and.

Be it resolved that the moment we gave either up or in has been appended

To our record's errata, archived as a correction to the long-form, full-text,

Unimpeachably original of our birth certificate, the ink of which no baptism

Could smear and no court expunge, the mark of an inhumanity so accidental,

Born of failure or exhaustion—how we're never not soaked in sweat anymore—

Or the inability to remember what other than this we would hope for or why,

A thing so trivial and so without intent it might well go entirely unnoticed,

As now so many things, details melting in a mass of indiscernible detail

So that eventually, what or who may or may not on or near the sidewalk,

Or else tucked in beneath or somehow sprawled into the bushes be dying

Cannot breach the protective Tyvek shell of that thing we've come to think of

As consciousness but which is really a progressive constriction not of the idea of

But of the actual world, which only caught my attention this morning

Momentarily and because it was so out of sorts with itself, the man not prone

Where he ought to be but in the street instead and wearing of all things

A suit and hat, as if this were half a century ago and he was his own father

And one could still go for a walk in the crisp air of whatever country

One was born in, and if one was drunk at so early an hour there was a romance

About it and not this piss-soaked and mumbling weight in my arms that I lift

Above the curb and to the grass and lean against a light post and keep walking,

Order restored: hope is a thing that falters, a feather fallen mucked in the

gutter.

In witness whereof God evolved from men and men, at bottom, from nothing

Much to speak of, heat mostly, and of accident some unknown measure

The after-the-fact interpretation of which reaches even now out toward us

As God's very hand, God's living hand, so much, it turns out, like our own

The two can hardly be distinguished as they train our sight where the horizon's

Hope of something else used to lie, the air there all the colors of a furnace

And the pointing finger not strained but casually authoritative, as if the fault

Were ours alone in that we simply had not looked hard enough,

Or in the right way, or in the way people are meant to look upon things,

Which is, the finger shows us, with a godlike confidence that there couldn't be

Anything else to see but this, and the unbearable heat of it, and the tragic

Accident of it not having to be at all are therefore neither unbearable

Nor tragic, but quite simply the nature of things, the guidance of God's hand,

And so excused utterly from fault in our deliberations, figured as constants

In our equations, which've widened now to enrobe the whole world hopelessly

In a code so binding, so intolerant of what cannot be figured in its terms

That we have at last no other option but to accept this idea that Pat Robertson's

Particular evil is either, at best, from fate inscribed in his gold-plated helices,

Or, at worst, the very good it claims to be, a possibility only imaginable

When one considers the slow but advancing progress of God's refinement

From a bituminous and crude idea of what's beyond the self yet somehow like it

To the self itself's finest distillate, a thing that can be splashed across the faces

And in the widened eyes of unbelievers and unclean women who congregate

Against, I would say, their will, were they allowed such an abomination,

In the ghettos ready-made for them near the city wall, the end's staging area,
A place only an asshole of the purest pedigree, the most precise extraction
Of the Robertsons, the McCarthys, of Ronald Reagan and J. Edgar Hoover,
And the process itself underwritten and undertaken by Exxon, by BP,
By Royal Dutch Shell at refineries retooled for the express purpose of it,
Of boiling off all but the essence of the men, of burning it off to provide us
Our Our Father, who anyway's mostly absent, who's present only in storms
And the methane flares that burn uselessly atop oil rigs, air bending
Behind them while the storm comes, then the rig inundated, the crude spilled
So that now, as we speak, the sea is on fire, and because with gulls and fish
And frogs and all manner of things God is angry, they are born clear or bent
Or without bones and in a lake of fire, which starts to sound ancient and isn't.

Be it resolved that the sky was once the vault of heaven, and could with a cold

Pull taut the everyday and preserve it that way, at least for a while in memory,

At least for a while while a memory of beauty in the everyday distracted us

From the other things, how our *never agains* had already grown empty, archaic,

A process that began as soon as they first echoed back to us, their few syllables

Unable to contain the past they papered over, the past they prettied up instead

With an endless succession of ribbon cuttings, endless unveilings

Of the clean angles and concrete courtyards of our Bureaus of Lessons Learned,

While, meantime, the sky, already fallen ill, already grown heavy with carbon,

Grown solid, and so grown useless for serving its purpose, for providing a space

Between all of this and something else, fell too into resignation and so out

Also of a job and into bankruptcy and so by court order was disincorporated,

Segmented out and sold at pennies on the dollar to creditors possessing

The necessary vision—a skill interested members of the business community

Can acquire at BLL-sponsored workshops, seminars, and weekend retreats—

To imagine it not as the useless and mute scrap of a useless and mute history

But rather as the necessary raw materials for whole series of heat-processed

By-products, sterile stuff that's used as fillers, as preservatives and adjuncts,

Stuff even this morning we ate without knowing in our breakfasts or smeared

And then massaged into our skin, which, *inexplicably,* we say, has blistered,

And has once and for all left all of its capillaries dilated in a useless attempt

To cool us with the means nature left us, which were enough once, long before

All our burnt offerings summoned finally the hell we had so long dreamt of.

Submitted respectfully and read into record on this Day of Our Lord—
And we would be remiss at this point not to at least mention our debt
To the coked-up, chest-thumping, junior disciples of whatever few brokerages
Still exist, their tireless striving to welcome us all into their flock,
To find a value in all we do, for having determined at long last respect's
Precise worth, for having rendered it available in the sort of modest
Denominations that are within reach of all, and to which anyway
We are accustomed: sensibly low word and character counts, reasonable
Restrictions on multi-syllabics and subordinate clauses, forms of mourning
That facilitate closure, the mourning industry's industry-standard content—
And on this Day of Our Lord entered into the archives and sealed
While we must yet go on, Brothers and Sisters and Little Babies, must yet
Bear the responsibility of going on, of rebuilding our lives, and of parting
The burning waters or burning the parted waters or whatever was our calling,
Something seeming to have been calling us here to do something, some voice
In the air where there was once just emptiness, where there was once nothing,
Which is beyond contempt, Little Babies, and this is something you too in
    time
Must learn, in a future bright as the strike of iron against flint and expanding
Brightly as the preemptive strike we must make against our enemies,
Whose country is hot and dry, more so even than ours, and who are hungry,
And who are coming and must be stopped, whose threat will require us
To sacrifice, to build, to press into that future and let what is past pass,
Let it recede from us further, and farther, and faster still until nothing's left

But a point, nothing but a memory of a star we could once see rising

Behind some palms' black silhouettes, that troubling sense of space, of

    stillness,

But somewhere, and before it goes to commercial again, a radio reassuring us,

A radio amplifying the voice of what's in the air, what's been in the air

For so long now, though surely before this there must've been something else

On our minds: *come on come on and dance all night; despite the heat it'll be*

    alright.

For those in need, grief counseling will be available for a nominal fee.

& PLAYS IT ONE MORE TIME, WITH FEELING, IN THE ROTATING PIANO BAR ATOP THE GRAND HOTEL ABYSS

a folie à deux & a defense of poetry

I am mad for it to be in contact with me.

—Whitman

More happy love! more happy, happy love!

—Keats

Distrustful of crowds, distrustful of the sing-along's easy populism, he sips,
Solitary, at whiskey and fiddles the damp cocktail napkin's disintegration—
Rolls little severed limbs of it in memoriam the war, rolls earthworms

And nematodes and centipedes in memoriam the living Earth's transposition
Into the Earth that is dying, and not only it but also all that must with it
Die too and transpose itself then into dead Earth and—, and all while

He tries, in a way that's beginning, you think, to look desperate, or worse,
Forced, contrived, to figure his way into, and then immediately out of,
The next phrase. He seems somehow so certain the right combination's

Possible, so certain it's there, waiting to be teased out and released
Of itself, so sure that, given time, he could find it. Even ignoring the others,
This alone is reason enough not to like him, he—arrogant prick—who would

Presume to know the score, while, eighty bleached-sheet and tight-tucked
Stories below that revolving lounge's come-back-round-into-fashion-at-last
Décor, its dizzying view, the rest of us are still living moment-to-moment

In a moment that, so far, has refused to either come to some merciful end
Or get around to anything we would want to call a meaningful start.
And when it became clear to us that something had to be done, from him

What but more nothing, more doodling, more scratching at idea's edge?
Of all our voices we have now made one voice, of all our aimless amblings,
The March of History. Isolated, out-of-touch, what could he know

Of how it felt when things suddenly, gradually, became so terrible that taking
En masse to the streets, the sidewalks, the public parks' anachronistic shade,
Started to seem like a good idea? Ignorant of the discomfort of conforming

One's back to the bus bench's unconformable contours, tinkering through
His piddling melodies—and they're never even the nice sort of thing a person
Could follow, never the songs in which you so immediately recognize yourself

You may have known them all along, memorized or somehow pre-populated,

And so you whistle them as signals to comrades, to allies and confederates

As signals for what we and it and no one else know must surely come—,

He doesn't know shit. Is hardly even alive. And hell, a lot of us

Have the feeling, having weathered so many years of this—all of them

Hot ones—that it's going to pick up. But because I once saw him

With a look of such shock, such despair, his eyes having seemed

To widen beyond themselves, his lips just slightly apart and so the tips

Of his teeth drying in the air, give him, for my benefit, the benefit

Of the doubt as we begin to enter, as if such a thing were possible,

His consciousness a little more closely as he clutters through

This attempt at composition, tries first this note, tries next that:

Dear Sentence, Dear Word, Dear Arrangement of Nothing Against

Nothingness, I was feeling bad about the note on which our last

Conversation ended, was feeling, you know, I'd been unfair in what I said,

All those things I said which were, I know, once again far less about the *you*

I used to refer to you than they were about me—my reluctance, my distrust,

My checking once more the balance of my checking account or thinking

About a little music or whether I ought or not to order another drink

While we were, by all accounts, trying to have a sort of moment,

A moment, forgive me, I've by now entirely forgotten the content of—,

And this would, I think, have all been clear enough if it weren't for my

Bad habit of saying *he* as regards the man I have sometimes also referred to

As *the man* instead of the *I* I intend or would intend if its use didn't make

Everything sound so deliriously awful, so near to me as I try to get

Near to it, but what I mean now is that he was sorry, the man was sorry,

And I am too, a sorry man, and older too now and wizened inside of it,

In the onslaught of it, how every morning you wake, you know, again in it,

And how its routine masks the other of it, the startled shock of feeling

Everything all at once, stars dying and people too, even and more often now

The people you have known, the those you knew, and children born

Into what will become for them the only horror they know, the only thing

They know, and even the little bits of beautiful things they will find

Sometimes along the roadside as they evacuate first this city, then that—

Some pebbled safety glass a Mediterranean in miniature and pixelated

And scattered like a handful of wheat or something nourishing and not

A trace of who was flung through it and out into the Vast Who Knows?—,

How even what they will want to take comfort in must not be modulated

Into what comforts, must not become another among the lies we sing

To make ourselves feel better, to distract ourselves from the fact that this

Cannot continue, that we cannot survive and certainly those others

Out beyond our imagination's reach cannot survive another of these

Pathetic and extraordinarily clunky renditions of atrocity's aftereffects,

The grass growing back thicker this time and greener too, fed

By the nitrogen-rich blood of those dead and everyone else having learned

Some wholesome lesson, having reaped some fulsome and nourishing

Harvest of wisdom that might be carried, as if in a handwoven basket,

Out of the fields and past the farmhouse and into the blinding future,

Which blinds them, which blisters their backs even from this distance

As they turn, this distance which has already pressed them into its service,

Which, in its infinite wisdom, consumes them and has absorbed them

Into that which falls under the name of living, a dissolution of us

Into what is not us exactly and is not others either but is a storm

We are always in the eye of, always in the closing and delirious eye of,

So that whichever way you turn your back is to it and whichever way
You walk you walk toward it, or I do, I mean, or we do, or that's what
I meant to say to you, anyway, that you're here in it too with me,
Whether you or I or he or it likes it, whether we might legitimately
Like to be left alone, to keep ourselves to ourselves and not become
Servants to some other thing, not because we shouldn't desire it,
But because that song's been over all our lives, and whistling its
Recapitulation or humming its bridge as you walk to the barricades
Is already your capitulation, your agreement to become another thing,
And while it may have been madness to recognize any of this at all
It would be madder still to look away, to consent to this consumption—
As even in our lying memories now Keats, Severn there beside him
Dripping sweat all over his sketchpad, talentless and immune,
Did from within, or else as others from without, over and over
At the center of self-immolation's blaze, off to the side a gasoline can
Or whatever other accelerant could be sourced locally and cheaply
And without unduly drawing authorities' attention—, it would be mad
To want to be remembered as anything, maddest of all a martyr, maddest
Of all as a name that stands for something, becomes its own shorthand,
Its own corrosive little bit of wisdom whispered in the ears of children,
The hissing of its *forsake now children all of these your childish things*
Hissing still, hissing even now as you grow distracted in it, and you'll
Please excuse me, allow me to continue, to elaborate a little more fully,
Even as your checking account's balance weighs on your imagination,
Even as you begin to doubt the vaporous credentialing agency
Who vouches for the immaterial, electronic-only certificate granted
You upon your completion of Sensitivity Awareness Training,
Because your patience with me has begun to chafe against all your
Better instincts, and you've been kind, sensitive, I know you've been,

But I want to say this now and as well as I can because I'm worried

We don't yet have time on our side: Darling, Dearest, *Principii Delirium,*

Principii Lex, we've got to stop calling everything by its wrong name,

Got to stop repeating every time we speak with each other

The wrong names that we've given things—martyr and hero and

Villain and wisdom and evil—, and even you, Dear Sentence,

Dear Word, Dear Arrangement of Nothing Against Nothingness,

Even though, it's true, I find you enchanting, we must nonetheless

Recite—in full—the whole of your name, must continue the chant of it

Until its spell breaks open and the gasoline either you or I or he or we

Splashed into your face onto your clothes and the quick of the match

Is extinguished in you, becomes disenchanted of its task, tired

Of always turning one thing into another, by force, by heat,

By the breaking of bonds which hold us together, we must continue

Until you are no longer a sacrifice, until the chant no longer sacrifices

You so that then enchantment and walking down the street or waiting

For the bus or reading long and late and waking, later, to it slowly again

And the light it casts then through the curtains' gauze will all belong

Once more to each other, and we'll speak of everything in the genitive,

Speak everything in the possessive until by virtue of having everything,

Everything possesses nothing and has also nothing's pear blossoms

And nothing's lovely little smile, which looks for a moment

Out of the corner of my eye like a town I grew up in once,

Looks like the town before I knew it well, its strip malls and dust

And how it seemed my parents had lived their whole lives there,

Which more or less they had, having not had to make a run for it,

Having not had to flee, having not had to forget, having not had

To become so numb to its passages, its passing, its always-just-out-of-

Grasp-ness, and in its lovely little smile my grasp on nothing begins

To loosen a little now and relax, begins to lean on what is not it,

Which leans back and like a child whistles nothing to no one

Or hums it otherwise and follows it, and lets it follow, and walks

A little further, and as if there were no need for hope, the child

Follows no hope, but only walks and whistles its unending name,

Whistles what could continue, what could go on without repeating,

Not other than itself, not not the whole of it and not, either, the whole,

And look at how it moves with itself, how it moves of its own accord,

It moves in accord with itself and even when it ends it will not.

NOTES

"Stare Decisis et Non Quieta Movere"—The Latin translates as "Stand by what is decided and do not disturb what is settled," which is closely aligned with the English idiom "Let sleeping dogs lie." As a legal principle, stare decisis refers to the necessity that judges respect precedent.

Bush spake this particular gem of an epigraph in an interview with Bob Woodward, who is also an asshole, but of a different stripe.

In Platonic and Gnostic thinking, the Demiurge is the universal creative force; the Greek translates literally as "public worker."

Apologies to Mssrs. Stevens and Hass for the thefts.

"Habeas Corpus"—The title translates as "You have the body." The writ of habeas corpus, often referred to as the Great Writ, seeks to guarantee against unlawful imprisonment by obligating authorities to produce the accused in court.

United States v. Lyons: 731 F.2d 243, 739 F.2d 994 (1984)

Apologies to Mr. Roethke.

"Civil Twilight"—The title refers to the times of morning and evening when the sun has either not yet crossed above or has already crossed below the horizon, during which time light from the sun is still sufficient to clearly distinguish objects and surroundings under normal weather conditions.

It was actually a member of the French National Assembly who, in 1851, used the term "anti-riot streets," and Napoleon III's Prefect of the Seine Department, Baron Haussmann, who included them in his massive renovation of Paris.

Apologies to Mr. Eliot's draft titles.

The epigraph is from an April 7, 1970, meeting of the California Council of Growers. Reagan, then governor of California, was responding to a question regarding how to deal with the protests in Berkeley and the East Bay. His press secretary later claimed that he only meant it as a "figure of speech."

I have never in fact seen Reagan's movie *Bedtime for Bonzo* (1951).

"Deleted Scene"—Epigraph from Levis's "Caravaggio: Swirl & Vortex" and in memoriam analog broadcast television, d. June 12, 2009, at the hands of the Digital Transition and Public Safety Act of 2005; duck cooked medium rare and served with polenta and roasted figs.

This poem's reference to the movie *Top Gun* (1986) is, rest assured, an embarrassed one.

"Offering of Two Burning Calves"—In memoriam my 1964 Ford Galaxie, d. 1997. "Me and Bobby McGee" was written by Kris Kristofferson but most famously performed by Joplin.

"Sort of Like, Um, the Falcon & the Falconer or Whatever, but Sort of Not"— Dedicated to the student who uttered the title phrase in class and who, sadly, I've otherwise forgotten. Epigraphs obvious.

"Resolution in Loving Memory of Sky & Gooseflesh"—Epigraphs from Baudelaire's "To Every Man His Chimera," Robert Hullot-Kentor's essay "Critique of the Organic: Kierkegaard and the Construction of the Aesthetic," from *Things Beyond Resemblance,* and Dickinson's #314 from *The Poems of Emily Dickinson Edited by R. W. Franklin.*

Apologies to Mr. Keats and The Lovin' Spoonful.

"& Plays It One More Time, with Feeling, in the Rotating Piano Bar atop the Grand Hotel Abyss"—Georg Lukács accused Theodor Adorno of having "taken up residence in the 'Grand Hotel Abyss' which [he] described in connection with [his] critique of Schopenhauer as 'a beautiful hotel, equipped with every comfort, on the edge of an abyss, of nothingness, of absurdity. And the daily contemplation of the abyss between excellent meals or artistic entertainments can only heighten the enjoyment of the subtle comforts offered.'"

The rotating BonaVista Lounge, which sits atop the Westin Bonaventure in downtown Los Angeles, supplied some springboard for the imagined setting, though it's important to note that while the lobby bar in the Bonaventure does offer live piano music, the BonaVista has, in fact, no piano. At both the lobby bar and the BonaVista, patrons are offered a glass of classic Chex Mix with their drinks, a gesture that seems strikingly like poor consolation for something.

Apologies to Mssrs. Stevens and Everwine. Apologies, in fact, all around.

The National Poetry Series was established in 1978 to ensure the publication of five collections of poetry annually through five participating publishers. The Series is funded annually by Amazon Literary Partnership, Barnes & Noble, Betsy Community Fund, the Gettinger Family Foundation, Bruce Gibney, HarperCollins Publishers, Stephen King, Lannan Foundation, Newman's Own Foundation, News Corp, Anna and Olafur Olafsson, the O. R. Foundation, the PG Family Foundation, the Poetry Foundation, Laura and Robert Sillerman, Amy R. Tan and Louis De Mattei, Elise and Steven Trulaske, and the National Poetry Series Board of Directors.

THE NATIONAL POETRY SERIES
WINNERS OF 2016 OPEN COMPETITION

I Know Your Kind
William Brewer
Chosen by Ada Limon for Milkweed

For Want of Water
Sasha Pimentel
Chosen by Gregory Pardlo for Beacon Press

Civil Twilight
Jeffrey Schultz of Los Angeles, California
Chosen by David St. John for Ecco

Madness
sam sax
Chosen by Terrance Hayes for Penguin Books

Thaw
Chelsea Dingman
Chosen by Allison Joseph for University of Georgia Press